THE SEEK
CHALLENGE

ROCHELLE D. MASON

DEDICATION

To my mother, Rosie, who introduced me to Jesus and the Word of God. Listening to her pray each day and read her Bible showed me the reality of God. Christianity was not something she experienced on Sunday. Mom walked with Jesus every day. God used her to lead our family to Christ, and I am forever grateful for her love and her prayers that have carried us through. She's the absolute best—a mom after God's own heart.

"And ye shall seek me, and find me, when ye shall search for me with all your heart."

-Jeremiah 29:13

TABLE OF CONTENTS

ACKNOWLEDGEMENT

I would like to acknowledge the amazing team of people that helped with this project: my amazing friend and graphic designer, Latriya White, and my awesome editor Lisa Beasley. I also want to acknowledge my family, friends and my wonderful launch team for all their support (Michelle & Howard Harris, Lenzie Lucas, Oquendo Cofield, Dylan Hewitt, Destanie Spencer, Jill Ragland, Gwen Moore, Karima Davis, Melissa & Bryce Hancock, Marcus Lawrence and Twana & Fred Hall).

I also want to say thank you to my World Changers family (Pastor Alyssa Worrell, Pastors Michael and Shemika Owens, Pastors Archie & Melissa Collins, Minister Toya Exnicious, Janice Moreland, Pam Horton and Dr. Monica Hill) for all their love and support over the years. Thanks also to my spiritual parents, Pastors Creflo and Taffi Dollar, for teaching me the Word of God and for providing a wonderful church for me to learn and grow in the things of God.

INTRODUCTION

I struggled to write this book. I started and stopped many times because I was a serial procrastinator. I have always been a strong starter, but a finisher? Now, that's another story. This bad habit of mine started to frustrate me. I was tired of having all these ideas and plans I believed God had given me that I was NOT fulfilling. When I first got the idea for this book, I was driving down the expressway, and it flooded my heart. I was fired up. But eventually, as time went on, the fire fizzled out.

Several years later, I was in the bathroom at my friend's house, and the frustration hit me again. As I was thinking about The Seek Challenge, I heard God speak to me. He said, "You do it." In other words, He was saying He wanted me to do the seek challenge. He wanted me to go through the process of seeking Him so that I would be able to share my experience with you.

I knew He was talking about this book. I needed to write about it. So, I said, "Okay." After I said it, I felt a sense of inner excitement because I know from experience that, when we seek God, something good always comes out of it. But I had no idea that my life would change during the twenty-one days of the seek challenge. Everything I had been trying to do on my own was not working, but as I began to seek God, things started to change in my everyday life.

The Seek Challenge is not a fad; it's not a magic

trick. The number twenty-one is not a mystical number. Twenty-one days of seeking God is simply a God-centered goal. It's a starting point and stopping point to assessing the differences we see in our lives and in ourselves after pursuing a relationship with the Creator of all that is good. How could this be anything less than beautiful and exciting? I call it a challenge because this is something that should be done but may not be easy. The good thing is that most people like challenges, but this one requires focus. We are such a distracted generation. There are so many things competing for our attention. It's truly a struggle to focus on just about anything. Multitasking is the norm today. However, God tells us to seek Him first. And there's a reason for this: so we can win. He loves us, and He wants us to be successful in everything we do. He is the one who holds the power to success.

When I did the seek challenge, God transformed my failing life into a success. He brought my life into a season of promotion and independence. I was living at a friend's house, up to my ears in debt and divorced, trying to live again after my life and heart had been broken into a million pieces. In twenty-one days, God promoted me on my job, increased my salary, helped me remove negative marks off my credit report, helped me move into a beautiful apartment with a paradise view, and showed me favor on every turn. Yes, He did all this in twenty-one days.

Ready, Set, Seek!

WHY SEEK GOD?

Why should anyone seek God? A lot of people may wonder what it even means to seek God and how can that help with the issues of everyday life. We all seek so many things: money, relationships, the right job, our purpose, sex, drugs, and fame, just to name a few. As human beings, we are always in pursuit of something, regardless of what we believe or what religion we adhere to. The thing that I have realized is that seeking God is the most valuable and beneficial thing we can do because He is the creator of all things. Every good thing we could ever desire in life comes from Him. One of God's names is Jehovah Jireh, which means "provider," or "the Lord will provide," in the Hebrew language. That very descriptive name tells us that, no matter what our need may be, God has the supply and will give it to us. I love Psalm 23 because that entire psalm talks about God's provisions for us, even in the worst circumstances.

Verses 1-3 are my favorite part of the psalm:

The Lord is my Shepherd [to feed, to guide and to shield me],
I shall not want.
He lets me lie down in green pastures;
He leads me beside the still and quiet waters.
He refreshes and restores my soul (life);
He leads me in the paths of righteousness
for His name's sake (AMP).

When Moses met God for the first time, Moses asked God "What is your name?" God said, "I AM that I AM." God is. Period! Whatever we need, God is. It's all in Him. It really makes sense, because He is the one that breathed the breath of life into us. He made everything that we see, everything that helps us to create and sustain life. Without Him, we couldn't do a thing. When we really humble ourselves and see things as they are, we can realize that we don't have all the answers. And, therefore, we need God.

There are many things we can reach out for that can give us pleasure, enjoyment, and temporary feelings of contentment, but what do we do when those things no longer satisfy? What do we do when we feel emptiness and hurt so deeply that nothing helps? It is often when we are at that point that we reach out to God. If we don't reach out to God, we often turn to other people, sex, drugs, alcohol, work, and anything else we can think of. And guess what happens after that? Fallouts, addictions, and all kinds of other negative things occur, simply because those "other things" don't satisfy and fill the void we desire to fill.

If you look at people who struggle with addictions and other negative habits, they are usually in pursuit of something they lack, and they are desperately trying to obtain it—be it comfort, love, security, etc. It's basically like the song says, "looking for love in all the wrong places." I'm here to tell you that God is the right place. I am not telling you that seeking God will make your life perfect. Oh no, I'm not going to lie to you. I do know from experience that God is the only one who can get you through the worst of times, and He is the only one who can make impossibilities possible. He's the miracle worker when you need one. He's the one who saves us when we're drowning. I know because He has saved me from depression, death, unbearable heartache, and probably evils I don't even know about. He's the person you want to know when your back is up against the wall. He said, when we seek Him with all our hearts, we will find Him. Let's seek God together. He's waiting, and He wants to be found.

For I know the plans and thoughts that I have for you, says the Lord, plans for peace and well-being and not for disaster, to give you a future and a hope. Then you will call on Me and you will come and pray to Me, and I will hear [your voice] and I will listen to you. Then [with a deep longing] you will seek Me and require Me [as a vital necessity] and [you will] find Me when you search for Me with all your heart (Jeremiah 29:11-13, AMP).

Now that we understand why it's important to seek God, it's now time to do it. Here are some easy and practical steps toward getting started:

•**Find a quiet place.** It can be your bathroom or bedroom, or by a lake or in a park. It really doesn't matter where, just a place where you can quiet your mind and focus.

•**Bring your Bible and a note pad**. The Bible is God's letter to us, and it helps us get to know Him better. With the note pad, you can write down whatever you believe God is saying to you and refer to it later.

•**Read something.** Reading the Bible will help you to recognize the "tone" of God's voice and how He speaks. Read something simple, like a Psalm, for starters, just to help focus your mind on God.

•**Talk.** Say something like, "Father, I come to You in the name of Your Son, Jesus, and I want to get to know You more. Speak to me, lead me, and guide me. Help me to know You more and develop a strong relationship with You." It doesn't have to be these exact words, but it's a good start.

•**Listen.** After you pray, listen. That is the polite thing to do, right? God really wants to speak to you. It could be a thought, an idea, a soft voice, or just a sense of love and warmth all around you. God is very creative and loving, and He knows exactly how to communicate with His children. All He needs is a listening ear and an open heart.

Ready, Set, Seek!

Record your experience with God.

What is your prayer?

What do you believe God is saying to you?

DAY TWO

WHAT DOES IT MEAN TO SEEK GOD?

What does it mean to seek God? How do you look for the Creator of the universe, an invisible God who has never been seen? How do you know when you have found Him? These are all very valid questions. I love words, and I love looking them up to get a deeper meaning of them. So I looked up the word "seek" in the dictionary and found this definition: "to go in search or quest of: to seek the truth; to try to find or discover by searching or questioning; to seek the solution to a problem; to try to obtain" (Dictionary.com).

One of the Hebrew words for seek is zeteo, which means "to seek by inquiring; to investigate, to reach a binding (terminal) resolution; to search, 'getting to the bottom of a matter'" (Biblehub.com).2 Basically, to seek God means to ask Him questions, go after Him, research Him, investigate Him, set up a meeting with Him, communicate with Him; to desire Him. The awesome thing about seeking God is that this quest comes with a promise: When we seek God with all our hearts, we will find Him.

Questioning God is something that many religious people say we should never do. They say that questioning God is disrespectful and blasphemous, but that is the opposite of what God says. God wants us to inquire of Him and require Him as our most vital necessity. He wants to give us wisdom and reveal to us secret things. I like what

Jesus said in Matthew 7:7.

"Ask and keep on asking and it will be given to you; seek and keep on seeking and you will find; knock and keep on knocking and the door will be opened to you" (AMP).

If we want to find God in a real, authentic way and have an authentic experience with Him, we must put forth some effort. I believe that many people are quick to say that God isn't real or that they don't need Him because they have not taken time to get to know who He is. In essence, they have "judged" God and sized Him up based on someone else's interpretation or experience with Him, or lack thereof. We don't like to be judged; yet at times, we judge our Creator and fail to find out who He really is. That is when we lose.

When we look at God from the standpoint of His main point of reference, which is His Word (the Bible), we see that He is the wisdom giver. Check out what James says:

"If any of you lacks wisdom [to guide him through a decision or circumstance], he is to ask of [our benevolent] God, who gives to everyone generously and without rebuke or blame, and it will be given to him" (James 1:5, AMP).

If you want to know the answers to real-life questions and situations, consider James' advice, which is to ask God. He is all-knowing. He knows the future, and He see the hearts of all men. Yet, we try to figure these things out with limited knowledge and resources. God loves us so much, and He wants to take the struggle and stress out of our daily lives. That is why He invites us to "ask." God always has a solution to every situation we face. There is no such thing as impossibilities with God.

Do something different today. Light a candle; put on some worship music. I listen to Hillsong Worship a lot. Pandora and Apple Music are music apps that will pull up a great worship play list. Begin thanking God for all the good things in your life and ask Him to help you get to know Him better, and then go for it. Talk to Him and give Him a chance to talk to you. Remember, anything you hear from Him will be good, will bring peace, and will line up with the Bible. Be sure to end your time of worship with prayer!

Ready, Set, Seek!

Record your experience with God.

What is your prayer?

What do you believe God is saying to you?

HOW TO STAY FOCUSED

Focus is the key to any successful endeavor. If you were searching for gold, you would have to make sure you had all the proper tools, and you would have to spend a considerable amount of time digging and researching and sweating to get to that precious gold. Now, I am in no way saying that God is allusive or that He wants us to "work" at finding Him. I am simply saying that for us to contact our invisible God, we must focus on the idea and the pursuit of spiritual things. We are humans, and we live in a tangible world where everything can be seen, touched, felt, and heard. Because of this earthly preoccupation, our focus on something invisible can be easily lost. Many people fail to experience God and His presence because they are simply too busy. Our everyday routines keep us so consumed and preoccupied that many of us cannot even enjoy our own existence, let alone seek God's presence. God is a distinguished gentleman, and He will never force His way into our lives. James 4:8 emphasizes this point:
"Draw near to God, and he will draw near to you" (NKJV).

Let's look at some definitions:

Distraction: A distraction is something that takes your attention away from what you're supposed to be doing (Vocabulary.com).

Preoccupy: Things that preoccupy you engross or enthrall you—they suck up all your attention and energy, sometimes to an unhealthy degree (Vocabulary.com).

Focus: Focus is something that camera lenses and sleepy students are always being asked to do. For cameras, it means finding a point where the subject is clear or "in focus." For students, it means paying attention.

"Focus is all about finding a center of a parabolic curve, of a lens, of a meditative state. In Latin, focus means 'domestic hearth,' which goes to show that not much has changed, since kitchens remain the focus of the modern home. Focus can be used as a verb, as in 'I need to focus on my work, so I can play video games later' and as a noun, as in 'What is the focus of this essay? I can't tell, since the writer seems to be all over the place'" (Vocabulary.com).

It takes focus to slow down and set aside time on a daily basis to seek after God. When you begin to do this, you will see the benefits, and the blessings you will experience will motivate you to continue. But just like anything good for us, seeking God takes effort and a willingness to prioritize it above other things in our lives. I must admit that writing this book was a huge challenge because of my lack of focus. I knew I needed to write the book, and I knew that it would benefit many people. I would be obeying God and opening the door to the life of my dreams by writing it. But guess what happened to me regularly when I thought about writing? Distraction. I got off focus every time until I decided to hold myself accountable to someone else and get it done.

I told my friend Shelly that I needed to be accountable to her while I wrote, and I also set a deadline. Taking those steps forced me to get on the ball.

Finding a "seek partner" may prove to be beneficial to you as well. A seek partner is someone you can pray with. You and your seek partner can encourage each other to seek after God. I have done this many times and it has been tremendously beneficial. Jesus even asked His disciples to wait and pray with Him, and the prophet Daniel had friends that prayed with him, especially in some very dire circumstances. Sometimes, having a partner really helps you to press into the presence of God and to fight those distractions so you can really focus. Just make sure your partner (or partners) has the same fervent desire to seek after God that you do. If you are someone who needs or prefers to be alone to really focus, that's fine too. The Bible mentions several times that Jesus would often go off by himself to pray.

"But Jesus would often go to some place where he could be alone and pray" (Luke 5:16, CEV).

Jesus was obviously sought after and was very busy. To ensure that He had His very necessary time with God, He went off by Himself to pray and gain strength and instructions on how to fulfill His destiny. We are not smarter than Jesus. If He had to do these practical things to help Him stay focused and pray, we can learn from His example.

•Pick your secret place. It can be a room, bathroom, park, etc. Wherever you can focus is where you will experience God so much more.

• Make a list of the things that distract you the most and determine the best time for you to steal away from those distractions and pray.

• If you need a partner, write down the name of someone you think will be a good fit and call him or her to set up your prayer plan.

• Pray

Ready, Set, Seek!

Record your experience with God.

What is your prayer?

What do you believe God is saying to you?

WHO SOUGHT GOD AND WHY?

Many people throughout history have sought after God. Who created the universe? Why are we here? What is the purpose of man's existence? All these questions have driven men and women all over the world to seek after the only one who can possibly have all these answers: God. God has been the mystery of the ages, and yet He is the most obvious being there is. It's very difficult to look at the world and outer space or even the miraculous birth of a child and think there is no God. I believe we all know deep inside that He is real, and there is an inner knowing that causes us to search. We search because we want to feel connected to Him, much like a baby longs for the touch of his or her mother. Something in us knows that, when we find God, we will finally be satisfied.

Oftentimes, when people sought after God, they were misled. The longing inside their souls drove them to search for the love of God in all the wrong places. Many people search for peace, love, and acceptance that only God can give. On their frantic search, they find drugs, alcohol, pornography, unhealthy relationships, money, fame, etc., and these things seem to provide a temporary sense of relief from this longing. Yet the longing returns, and they search and search again. Unfortunately, this search can lead to death, because all these "other things" cannot satisfy. People drown themselves in these substances and situations, seeking more in life. Instead, these things drain the life out of them. I believe this is why God says to love the Lord your God with all your heart, mind, soul and strength. When our love and devotion are focused on Him (the true life-giver), we will not be in danger of being drained lifeless by these empty substitutions for God. He wants you whole and full of life and love. He wants you to enjoy life the way He planned it—abundantly, to the full, until it overflow according to John 10:10 (AMP). There is no viable way to experience that kind of life without seeking God because He is the originator of all that is good.

Ready, Set, Seek!

Record your experience with God.

What is your prayer?

What do you believe God is saying to you?

AMAZING THINGS WILL HAPPEN!

When I was in the process of writing this book, I got stuck. I got preoccupied with life and all my issues, and writing this book became a distant yet nagging desire. I knew I had to do it, and I wanted to. But I just wasn't in the right frame of mind to do it. One day, as I was thinking and talking to God, I heard Him say, "You do it." I knew what He was talking about. God was telling me that I had to do the seek challenge first. Then I would be able to effectively write about it. It was almost as if I needed to prove it to myself, and then I would have something to say. Sure, I had put myself on a prayer mission before and seen results, but nothing like this. I had never done it so that I could share the results with the world. So, I started.

First, I set aside time just to focus on God. My usual routine had to be changed. I would usually pray "on the go," like in the car, in my head, or as needed, like most people do. But I had to do something different, so I chose to focus. I set aside ten to fifteen minutes each day just to focus completely on God. I would sometimes light candles, play relaxing worship music, and just start thanking God for His blessings. Then I would simply talk to Him about what was on my mind—my hopes, things I needed to do, and things that worried me. I asked Him to get involved. I started to tell Him about things that I was dealing with and the fact that I wanted to fulfill my purpose. That's when He told me that my purpose was to seek after Him, and as I did, I wouldn't have to worry about anything because He would work things out for me. He said my job is to be with Him, and He will work out the details of my life. It's not easy not to worry but staying in contact with God renews your trust and faith in knowing that He loves you.

I remember one day when my mom shared this scripture with me about seeking God and His Kingdom first, and then everything I need will be added:

Seek the Kingdom of God above all else, and live righteously, and he will give you everything you need (Matthew 6:33, NLT).

I knew she was right. To my surprise, I drove by a church not long after that which had that very message on its announcement board. That was another confirmation for me about seeking Him.

So, I did the seek challenge, and my life changed in twenty-one days. Things I had been trying to do suddenly started to work because I was no longer the one doing those things. I started to focus on God, and that enabled me to start seeing the power of God work in my life. I had recently gone through a very difficult divorce during that time, and everything in my life was in shambles. Before I did the seek challenge, I was trying to get promoted at work, so I could make a certain amount of money and get an apartment and start over. My credit was in horrible shape, and I was in a space where I felt like nothing was working for me, no matter how hard I tried.

After I started the seek challenge, it was like someone turned the light on, and things started to work out. I got a promotion, I got approved for an amazing apartment, and I received an $8,000 raise. It was amazing, and the timing of everything was perfect. I could not have planned it all if I had tried. I didn't even really know what was going on. I was just seeking after God daily, talking to Him about everything on my mind, praising Him, and simply staying aware of His awesome presence. It truly changed my life.

I believe that God wants to give us experiences like this every day, but we are so distracted that we can't even see His hands opened wide to us, filled with everything we want and need. During this time, my brother was going through the parole process, as he had been in prison for over twenty years. I told him about my experience with the seek challenge and asked him if he wanted to do the seek challenge with me. He said, "Let's start today!" He had been eligible for parole several times before, but each time he went before the board, they denied him. He decided to do the seek challenge, and my mom and sister did too. An amazing thing happened. My brother was approved for parole. After his attorney had come out of the hearing, she did not feel optimistic about getting a positive outcome. But God worked it out, and my brother was approved for parole!

When going into the seek challenge, you don't have to go in expecting anything specific. What is important is that your primary motive be to get closer to God and to experience more of Him. Receiving and experiencing good things is simply a bi-product of being close to Him. He is good, so goodness comes with Him. When someone loves you, that person looks for ways to make you happy. And God loves us more than we can ever imagine. So, it is to your advantage to get as close to Him as possible.

Taste and see that the Lord is good. Oh, the joys of those who take refuge in him! (Psalm 34:8, NLT).

This is a fantastic opportunity to talk to God about anything wrong in your life and to ask Him to get involved. He wants to. He's an expert at fixing things and making things beautiful again.

Ready, Set, Seek!

Record your experience with God.

What is your prayer?

What do you believe God is saying to you?

WATCH OUT FOR YOUR ENEMY

"Watch out for your enemy." That is an interesting title for a chapter; I know. But it is a fair and very valid warning. Whenever you are doing anything for God, your enemy—the devil—is on the prowl. The devil is no figment of our imagination. He's no scary character in a fairy tale. He is a real, living spirit that is the opposite of good, the enemy of light, and the biggest opposer to your success in life. He is the ultimate hater. He hates anything and everything that is connected to God, and if you are connected to God, that includes you. You are the object of the devil's hate because God is in love with you. You were made in God's image, and the Bible says that you are the apple of God's eye. The Bible also says that God is so enraptured by you that He has tattooed a picture of you in the palms of His hands.

Behold, I have indelibly imprinted (tattooed a picture of) you on the palm of each of My hands; [O Zion] your walls are continually before Me (Isaiah 49:16, AMP).

Can you believe that? Every time God uses His hands or even looks at them He's reminded of you. What an amazing thought—that the God who created the very universe loves us like that. What an amazing love!!! The awesome thing is this; because you know about God's love, you can also rest assured that God has your back and His eyes are always on you. In light of this love, you also must be mindful that you have an enemy who seeks to oppress and trap you. You must be careful not to fall into his traps.

One of the devil's biggest traps that he sets for God's beloved is busyness and distraction. By getting you caught up in everyday chores, errands, and activities, the devil hopes that you will forget about seeking God. If the devil can distract you long enough to create some distance between you and your heavenly Father, your Counselor, your Guide, and your Shield, he can then pounce on you. The devil knows that when you are disconnected from your life source you become weak.

God never leaves us; He never forgets about us. we are free, moral agents so we must stay connected to Him and remain focused on Him on purpose so that we can stay in the safe zone, where God is. Seeking God doesn't ensure that you will never have any trouble, but I can assure you that if you are in close contact with Him, you will always be delivered from the trouble if you have confidence and believe it in your heart.

Imagine a sheep and his shepherd are walking in the dark woods. Wolves are prowling around everywhere, hungry for their next meal, and you (the sheep) are in their range of scent. The only thing that deters them is the Shepard and His staff that He uses to guide and protect His sheep. You are walking close to your Shepherd when suddenly you see a rabbit scampering by, and you wonder where it's going. Now you are distracted, and you lag behind, slowly following behind the rabbit. Before you know it, you are alone in the dark woods, not because your Shepherd left you, but because you wandered off in the opposite direction. Now you are alone and gripped by fear because you don't know what to do, and everything is going wrong.

You are cold, hungry, and tired, but you can't rest because now you hear the wolves howling in the night. They are now closer than you've ever sensed or heard before. Your Shepard knows you are missing, and He's

23

calling out to you. But you are so far in the woods that you can't hear Him. All you hear is the howling wolves. But your Shepherd has keen hearing, and He knows the sounds of His sheep. Finally, you cry out, and your Shepherd comes running, with His staff, and fights off those wolves that were just about to have you as their next meal. Now you are safe in His arms again, just like the scripture says:

God is our mighty fortress, always ready to help in times of trouble. (Psalm 46:1, CEV).

This scenario reflects what tends to happen in our lives when we get lured too far away from our Shepherd, in the dark woods of depression, fear, despair, grief, and loneliness. Some people live in these conditions all their lives until they are consumed, or the darkness fills them and they begin to consume others like a wolf. We don't have to go down that path of distractions. My mother always tells me to **"stay focused,"** and now I understand why. Proverbs 4:27 says "not to look to the left or right and remove your foot from evil, (don't go off in the way of distractions). Stay focused on your God." The book of Daniel talks about how those who know their God will be strong and will take action. That is what The Seek Challenge is all about. When YOU know your God, you can take proper actions and change your life and then go out and change the world.

In your prayer time, bind up the enemy and every force he tries to send to harm you. Jesus said it best:

Verily I say unto you, whatsoever ye shall bind on earth shall be bound in Heaven; and so whatsoever ye shall loose on earth shall be loosed in Heaven (Matthew 18:18, KJ21).

Ready, Set, Seek!

Example prayer: *Father, in the name of Jesus, I bind the devil and every negative force that tries to come against me and Your awesome plan for my life. I loose blessings, prosperity, peace, and every good and perfect gift that You have for me.*

Record your experience with God.

What is your prayer?

What do you believe God is saying to you?

26

JESUS WAS A SEEKER

Jesus was a seeker. Think about that. The Savior of the world—Emmanuel, God with us—was a seeker. He made it a part of His everyday life because He understood our earthly plight. Jesus understood that, to make it in this shadowy world and to fulfill His mission, He had to seek after God. I know it was a challenge for Him at times. The Bible talks about how Jesus was "touched with the feeling of our infirmities." That basically means that He knew what it felt like to be tired, weak, distracted, saddened, depressed, disappointed, and tempted. He felt it all. **Jesus understands every weakness of ours, because he was tempted in every way that we are. But he did not sin! (Hebrews 4:15, CEV).**

He experienced all emotions and temptations, but he never failed or faltered. Of course, we know the main reason was because He was God in the flesh, but another reason He was strong was because He sought after God. He stayed in the safe zone. Even amid the enemy tempting Him right to His face, He won because He was focused on His God. Jesus even explained this, and how important seeking God is to the human experience. He said to always pray and be consistent. He said to stay in the face of God until you have built yourself up with His Word. When you spend time in God's word your faith will be strong, so you can walk in and exercise the power you already have inside of you.

I believe the biggest realization I've gotten out of seeking God is the realization that He's really with me—that He really loves me and has everything under control. I'm already blessed, successful, healed, and so much more. I just need to live in that reality. And being in His presence daily is the biggest reminder. Spending time with Him makes those amazing spiritual attributes more and more real until they manifest in your life.

Another cool thing that I have seen in the Scriptures is that Jesus showed us how to tap into the supernatural and how to have power for our purpose. It's through spending time with God. Jesus went around healing the sick, raising the dead, and reading people's minds, but even among the throng of followers and all the miracles, He refused to get distracted by the crowds, the fame, and the demands. Jesus would routinely go away by Himself and seek after God, receiving instruction, inspiration, and nurturance. He looked to God to get refueled and re-energized so that He could accomplish His mission and fulfill His calling: to serve and save humanity. If Jesus was a seeker, we should also be seekers. He said that we would do greater things than He did. How? By seeking and staying in His presence.

Ready, Set, Seek!

Record your experience with God.

What is your prayer?

What do you believe God is saying to you?

Ready, Set, Seek!

WEEK 1 COMPLETE!

DON'T LET YOUR FAILURES STOP YOU

Many people feel timid and out of their element when thinking about seeking God. Let me tell you; don't. God wants you as you are. No failure or short coming can stand in between you and your Father. Hebrews 4:16 tells us to come boldly to the throne of grace. What do we remember about grace? "Amazing grace, how sweet the sound that saved a wretch like me."

Jesus said, "Anyone who comes to me I will in no wise cast out" (John 6:37). No matter what you have been involved in, you are beloved by God. He's not surprised, grossed out or angry with you. When Jesus died on the cross, He covered you. He took on your sin and destroyed its power to separate you from God. Your sin has no power. It has no ability to keep you out of God's presence. Jesus cleared the way. He washed you with His blood. If you've received His invitation of salvation, you are good. You are on His ticket. So, come. Come as you are. God will take care of the details. Just come and keep coming with an honest and open heart, and He will surely be open and honest with you.

God loves you. Believe me; He loves you. He sent His precious Son to die for you so that you can be brought back to Him in love. Why would He reject you now? He's forgiven everything you have ever done wrong. It's okay. Just come.

Ready, Set, Seek!

This is your special time with God. Let God lead you as you pray.

If you have never received Jesus as your Lord and Savior, or if you are not sure, say this short prayer and mean it in your heart:

Lord Jesus, please come into my heart and save me. I ask for Your forgiveness of all my sins. I believe that You died on the cross for me and rose again on the third day.

I confess that You, Jesus, are Lord. I give my life to You, and I ask that You lead and guide me and help me to live for you each day. Thank You, Jesus, for saving me. Amen.

Record your experience with God.

What is your prayer?

What do you believe God is saying to you?

33

DAY NINE

CONSIDER FASTING

To many people, fasting seems like a spiritual ex-treme—something that "really spiritual" people do. It's also something that you don't hear much about. In our society, giving something up is not something that we are very excited about doing. Self-sacrifice is not appealing and is not a part of the everyday norm in today's society. Sure, we want to get all the results we desire, but giving up anything shouldn't have to be a part of the process. Being of this mindset and "never sacrificing" is where we miss it.

As we discuss seeking God, we must keep in mind that fasting has nothing to do with God hearing your prayers. Fasting is for your personal benefit and helps en-hance your ability to quiet your mind and spirit. The hu-man appetite is overwhelming, and it cries out to us every day. It is what we usually hear all day in our minds. We hear our hunger for food, sex, affection, and approval. We are driven by our appetites. But to have a more intimate and clear line of communication with God, it's important that we quiet all the "voices" of our appetites, worries, and fears and rise to a more focused awareness of God.

When Jesus went into the wilderness to seek God, He fasted for forty days. His mind and heart were clear and open to spiritual things. It is said that after fasting for a few days the body quiets down and feelings of hunger go away. I believe this is when our spirit becomes more "in control." For those of you who like scientific facts, let's take a look at some information about fasting:

34

An article from the John Hopkins Health Review states: "According to research conducted by neuroscientist Mark Mattson and others, cutting your energy intake by fasting several days a week might help your brain ward off neurodegenerative diseases like Alzheimer's and Parkinson's, while at the same time, improving memory and mood."

In different instances in the Bible, people have also fasted to show their sincerity in repentance, but we know that is not necessary now because Jesus paid the price for our sins. All we must do now is ask for forgiveness and receive it by His amazing grace. Fasting is now more so for us to "clear our spiritual ears," as my pastor says.

We can fast from many things other than food. We can fast from media, soda, sweets, etc. Fasting from anything that takes up a lot of your time and attention will only help in your pursuit of God and a deeper relationship with Him. I had a phenomenal experience with this in my teenage years.

I was very involved in my youth ministry, and there was an instance where I felt very strongly that God wanted our group to go on a collective media fast. I was about eighteen at the time, and I spoke to my assistant youth pastor about it. He told me that usually only spiritual leadership can call a fast in the church. But he believed that I had heard from God, so we did it. We didn't listen to any risqué music or watch any television for several days. It was decided that at the end of the fast, in our weekly midday service, we would all wear white to signify the end of our fast. It was amazing! The teens and the entire atmosphere of our ministry were different, and we really experienced the power of God in the service and in our ministry areas. Just imagine a group of teenagers seeking after God. It was a glorious experience.

God longs to be in relationship with us. When we draw near to Him, He draws near to us, and it delights

35

Him. We delight Him. God is more amazing and wonderful and more majestic and magnetic than we can ever imagine, and the more of Him you experience, the more you will want to experience. I imagine walking into a garden of wonder, and everything good that I can conceive is there. The deeper I travel inside of this garden, the more overwhelmingly wonderful it is. This is where I start to experience a river of goodness and desires being fulfilled.

Seeking after God comes with a promise that is found in another one of my favorite scriptures: "Delight yourself in the Lord, and He will give you the desires and secret petitions of your heart" (Psalm 37:4, AMP). It's like a beautiful dance with the lover of your soul. As you spend time in God's presence, His desires become your desires, and these right and purposeful desires begin to manifest in your life. I don't believe that my descriptions can do this justice. You must go in and experience all His goodness, healing, and love for yourself. Everything you need is found in His presence.

Ready, Set, Seek!

Record your experience with God.

What is your prayer?

What do you believe God is saying to you?

GOD SPEAKS

Prayer is not just talking to God. It also includes listening to God. Having a relationship with anyone is a two-way street. It's a dialogue between two individuals, sharing information, feelings, hopes, dreams, encouragement, love, etc. Have you ever talked to someone who never said anything back to you or who didn't acknowledge you at all? That is not a relationship and that is not what prayer and seeking God should be like. If it is, you are missing the whole point and most importantly you are missing out on God.

Many people are trained by religion to believe that God is some big being in the sky that just looks down on us and judges us and is not intimately involved in our lives. That is a false depiction of God. He sent His Son, Jesus, into the world and left letters about Him and His personality so that we can see what God is like. Think about it. God is the most creative, beautiful, and brilliant being that ever existed or that ever will exist. Everything wonderful in the world—everything complex and intelligent—was created, fashioned, formed and designed by Him. How can we sit in someone's presence that is so great and leave with nothing, leave with silence? When you are truly in His presence and have a heart to hear His voice, you will.

Can you imagine sitting with Oprah or any other great mind, but that person has nothing to say? I seriously doubt that would happen. When I think of people like Gandhi or Martin Luther King, Jr. or any other notable person, I would think that they are probably the most man-

nerable, humble and considerate people. I envision them having gentle and regal qualities; not pushy or aggressive. These people would probably wait for you to speak first, listen patiently and consider what you are saying. After listening to you, they would probably see into your soul as well. That is what God is like. Remember, He gave these great men and women their poise and wisdom. He created them and enabled them to accomplish all the amazing things they were able to accomplish. I am willing to bet that they would probably tell you that God gets all the glory for their
success.

We go into the presence of great men and women with a sense of awe and respect, and sometimes the first thing we say is how amazing they are and how we love their work. We gush and tell them how they've made a difference in our lives somehow. I'm sure that makes them feel pretty good. But, again, God created these people and this system of interaction, so shouldn't we go into God's presence with excitement and awe?

"Enter his gates with thanksgiving; go into His courts with praise; give thanks to Him and praise His name" (Psalm 100:4, NLT).

This is how we should enter into God's presence. I also like to say that praise gets God's attention. I'm not saying that He ignores us. But praise is almost like a cry of faith, where we are saying: "God, I acknowledge You and who You are and how great You are." Most people walk around ignoring God and disrespecting Him and all that He represents, and I am willing to bet that their lives demonstrate that same disrespect and defiance to everyone they meet. I have yet to meet someone who has a true relationship with God that acts ugly toward others. Those two concepts just don't go together. Talking to God and

39

praising Him changes us in so many ways, and intimate time focused on Him will make you even more sensitive to His voice and guidance, even when you are amid problems and noise.

When I was a teenager, I had a dream about walking through an outside mausoleum. I was all alone, and I had a very eerie feeling there. I began to see ghosts of people appear in the halls of the grave yard, and I became afraid and started to run. More ghosts started to appear, and I remembered the scripture that says, **But thou art holy, O thou that inhabits the praises of Israel (Psalm 22:3).**

In the dream, I knew, if I could get into God's presence, those spirits would have to leave. I began singing and praising God (while I was running). When I looked back, the ghosts started to disappear, and I felt safe again. That dream taught me that God loves me so much that He would remind me of how to access His presence and that being with Him will cause me to
triumph.

Praising God for your blessings and for who He is also lifts your spirit and puts you in a more positive and right frame of mind so that you can position yourself to hear His voice. He usually doesn't yell. He's very gentle and kind. And, because He knows you so well, He will speak to you in a way that you can understand. The most important thing to remember is to expect to hear, see, and feel. Expect to experience Him in some way.

God speaks in many ways. You may hear a voice, or thoughts or ideas may come to you that He inspires. You may dream, or He may speak to you through someone else. There are so many ways that He can get a message to you. It's very important to read the Bible to get to know more about how God speaks and how He thinks so that when you hear something, you can recognize if it's truly God or not. You can even ask Him to help you identify His voice more clearly, and He will help you. He's so awesome, and He loves you so much.

Ready, Set, Seek!

Record your experience with God.

What is your prayer?

What do you believe God is saying to you?

DON'T FORGET TO LISTEN

Listening is a lost art. Most people have no clue how to truly listen to a flesh-and-blood person, let alone to a God, whom they cannot see and touch. Listening is a hot commodity, so much so that people pay to have someone listen to them. That's what psychologists do all the time. They actually spend more time listening to what's being said and what's not being said to get to the heart of the patient and the heart of his or her issues. I have often heard that God gave us two ears and one mouth for a reason: so that we can listen twice as much as we talk. I believe that. Parents and children, husbands and wives, managers and employees, friends and family would all have much better relationships if we all would learn how to listen better.

I think sometimes it can get frustrating when it comes to seeking God because we may be looking for the big booming voice in the sky to tell us what to do and how to fix our lives, but we need to remember that God's attitude toward us should be observed and noted, because He's literally showing us how we should be. God is a gentleman, so He usually starts off listening. When He speaks, there is direct focus and results behind His powerful words. It is true that one word from God can change our whole lives, so we need to not only talk to God but also listen.

Now, don't get me wrong. He wants to hear from you. Sure, He knows your thoughts, and He knows what you are going to say before you say it. But He still wants to hear your voice because He's in love with you. He adores you. The sight of you makes His heart leap because you are His beloved. He loves you with an everlasting love that no one can even fathom—an amazing love. He wants to hear about your day and about what you are feeling. He wants you to share your life with Him, not only to hear you but also to help you. He wants you to cast your cares and concerns on Him so He can lead you to the solutions you need.

The only thing you really need to do is take your cares to Him, whatever you are dealing with, and He will orchestrate the answers and solutions. He's already done it. Think about every major problem you have faced. You really didn't know what to do. You may have tried different things but had no clue how things would turn out. We don't have all the answers. We can't even determine what will happen to us in the next five seconds, but God can. He holds the secret things and the future. All you need to do is let Him hold you, too, and trust that He's got you, because He does. The battle is believing in this truth so you can experience it. God's promises are true, but it's up to us to grab hold of them and be determined to live in them.

Listening to God is simple. After you have poured out your heart, just be quiet for a while. Sit in His presence like a student ready to be taught by the master teacher. It's a great idea to have a pen and pad so that you can take notes and make sure you don't forget. Moses was a good listener. He listened as God instructed Him on how to lead the children of Israel out of bondage. He listened when God gave him the Ten Commandments. He had to consult the Lord every step of the way, and He was there, every step of the way. Even when the people were crying out and behaving badly, God was there, comforting Moses and showing him the next steps.

Noah was also a good listener. He listened as God gave him the blue print, plans, and measurements for building the ark that saved his family and many animals so that life would continue after the flood. There are countless stories that can be told about the benefits of people listening to God. I can honestly say my biggest struggles in life ceased only when I got in the presence of my Father and heard His voice. That's when everything came together, when I was comforted, when my fears and worries went away.

Look at some of these promises from God and how great a listener He is when it comes to us:

> • This is the confidence that we have in Him, that if we ask anything according to His will he hears us (1 John 5:14, NIV).

> • Then you will call on me and come and pray to me and I will listen to you (Jeremiah 29:12, NIV).

> • I love the Lord for He heard my voice; He heard my cry for mercy. Because He turned His ear to me, I will call on Him as long as I live (Psalm 116:1-2, NIV)

> • In my distress I called to the Lord; I cried to my God for help. From His temple He heard my voice; my cry came before Him, even in His ears (Psalm 18:6, NIV).

> • In the morning, Lord, you hear my voice; in the morning I lay my requests before you and wait expectantly (Psalm 5:3, NIV).

> • The eyes of the Lord are on the righteous, and His ears are attentive to their cry (Psalm 34:15, NIV). Meditate on these promises and know that God is with you every step of the way.

Ready, Set, Seek!

Record your experience with God.

What is your prayer?

What do you believe God is saying to you?

Ready, Set, Seek!

THE HALF WAY MARK! KEEP SEEKING!

DAY TWELVE

WRITE IT DOWN

As I mentioned before, when spending time in the presence of God, having a pen and pad or taking notes in your cell phone (as long as it won't be a distraction) would be a good practice. One of my long-time ministry leaders used to tell us in ministry training that "anytime you are in the presence of a leader, always have a pen and pad." We are human. We forget things, even very important things, so we need to be able to document what God says to us so we can execute the directions we are given. Time with God is vital, and many times we have some very complex problems that we need guidance on. When God gives you guidance and direction, write it down.

I'm sure that, when Noah was getting all the measurements for the ark, he had something to record the information on. If not, something during the building process could have gone very wrong. When we are in God's presence, we must learn to take the experience seriously and really treat Him like He is real. We all really need to step up our reverence and respect for God and treat Him like the King that He is. He's not our errand boy. He's the King of Kings and Lord of Lords, and He deserves all the honor that we can give Him. Treat His words as gold and don't lose one. **And the LORD answered me: Write the vision; make it plain on tablets, so he may run who reads it (Habakkuk 2:2, ESV).**

God is about results. When He declares something, it will happen. God is more concerned about us doing what He says than merely hearing it. He tells us to be doers of the Word and not hearers only. No production

49

or results come from merely hearing. God wants us to have good, prosperous lives, and in order to experience that, we need to give Him attention and heed to His words of wisdom.

What do you believe you heard from God? Write it down.

Ready, Set, Seek!

Record your experience with God.

What is your prayer?

What do you believe God is saying to you?

BELIEVE THAT GOD IS IN LOVE WITH YOU

I can remember my mom talking to me about God when I was a child. As she spoke, I would always visualize God far above the clouds and even beyond outer space. I imagined that, after going to the end of outer space, suddenly everything would go white, and there heaven would be. Then we see God. I thought of Him as a giant, and usually all I could see was His feet and knees, while seated on His giant throne. As a child, I always felt like I knew Him somehow. He was always familiar to me. The thought of God being real was never far-fetched. I was quite passionate about believing in Him.

In Jeremiah 1:5, God is speaking to Jeremiah: **"Before I formed you in the womb, I knew you."** Despite this truth, many people don't see God as being with them or even knowing that they exist. We often think God is way up there somewhere looking down on us. But the truth is, He is not "way up there." He is here with us. Another name for Jesus is Emmanuel, meaning "God with us." His Word says that "He will never leave us or forsake us and that He will be with us until the end of the world" (Hebrews 13:5; Matthew 28:20).

The Bible talks about a friend that sticks closer than a brother and that the Spirit of God is in us. He's so close, as close as our heartbeats. He's on our side, rooting for us and believing in us. He knows who you are and what He put in you. He knows you are amazing, because He made you that way.

Seeking God is not about tracking His location, as

He is already with us. Seeking God is about being aware of His presence so that we can grow closer in our relationship with Him. At the other end of that relationship is all the goodness you can imagine. Psalm 34:8-9 says:

O taste and see that the Lord [our God] is good! Blessed (happy, fortunate, to be envied) is the man who trusts and takes refuge in Him.
O fear the Lord, you His saints [revere and worship Him]! For there is no want to those who truly revere and worship Him with godly fear (AMPC).

Taste, in this passage, is referring to trying God, experiencing Him, moving close to Him, and seeing Him for yourself. He wants to shower you with more love and goodness than you have ever known before. He wants you to Himself long enough to heal every pain and give you all the love and peace you can contain. He wants to cause you to recover from everything that the world has beat you up with. He wants to refresh and revive you and comfort you. Whatever you need, He wants to fulfill that need and bless you in ways you can't even fathom. He wants you to come to Him for this purpose, because He loves you so dearly and completely. Most of us have never seen love like this before, so it's hard to imagine. But that's why the scripture says to come "taste and see" (Psalm 34:8). Come and see. Draw near to God, and He will draw near to you. He can't wait for you to come into His presence so that He can show you His overwhelming love for you.

Zephaniah 3:17 says: The Lord your God wins victory after victory and is always with you. He celebrates and sings because of you, and he will refresh your life with his love" (CEV).

Many people believe that God is angry and disappointed in them, or He is waiting to strike us down. But that is a LIE. He sacrificed the most precious thing He had—His Son, Jesus—to get you back and to clear up everything that could separate you from His love. Jesus took all the excuses away—all the roadblocks, all the sins and shortcomings. All we must do is say "Yes, I'll come," and we can experience all the benefits of His love. God is mindful of you. He is always thinking of you, always aware of you:

Behold, I have indelibly imprinted (tattooed a picture of) you on the palm of each of My hands; [O Zion] your walls are continually before Me (Isaiah 49:16, AMPC).

Can you imagine that? Some people will tattoo a person's face or name on their body to demonstrate how intense their love is for that person. It shows devotion and passion, almost too much devotion. Seeing that makes me nervous because I'm thinking that, if the relationships don't last, they are stuck with the tattoo. But that is not the case with God. The love He has for us never wavers or ends. He has made up His mind about you, and His tattoo of you is staying right on the palms of His hands. He never takes His mind off you. Do you see how dynamic you are, that the Creator of the entire universe feels so deeply for you? Drink it in. It's all true.

Even though God has an amazing passion for you, He is a true gentleman. Therefore, He will not force His way into your life. He is very serious about your free will. He will never force His ways on you. He wants you to love Him and follow Him because you want to. He wants you to see the benefits for yourself and know that He wants the best for you. He's not trying to take from you; He's trying to give to you. He is love, and that is what love does. **The Lord appeared from of old to me [Israel], saying,**

Yes, I have loved you with an everlasting love; therefore, with loving-kindness have I drawn you and continued My faithfulness to you (Jeremiah 31:3, AMPC).

God's love for you is everlasting, meaning it will last forever, no matter what. He loved you even before you were born and He will always love you. He knows everything you will ever do and everything you will go through, and He loves you. No exceptions.

Ready, Set, Seek!

Record your experience with God.

What is your prayer?

What do you believe God is saying to you?

BE WILLING TO CHANGE

Change is a part of our existence. Some have said that it is the one constant in life. From the moment we are born until the moment we breathe our last breath, we are in the constant flow of change. We can see how natural it is because change is all around us, and it is displayed in everything. From the seasons of the year to butterflies, we are all agents of change. The interesting thing is that we often try to resist change. We fight change, and we get angry at change. But it's really a waste of time because as much as we dread it, we all change. What I am saying here is that, to really enjoy life and benefit from this amazing journey with God, we must be willing to change.

We should be willing to flow with God. He is always trying to help us to grow in maturity and wisdom and to expand our capacity to walk out all the magnificence He has placed in us. But for us to walk in our glory, we must change. My pastor says, "Change isn't change until you've changed." Psalm 55:19 says, "We have no changes because we fear not God." We are failing to respect God's design and plans when we refuse to change.

As you are on this amazing path of seeking God, He will often talk to you about changing—maybe changing your mindset, changing your eating habits, or changing how you think about and respond to others. My advice is this: Just go with it. Everything God leads and guides us to do is for our good and for the good of others. Change, in many cases, is good. Change, in many cases, represents growth. I really love how the Bible says that we go from "glory to glory." Imagine that. As you seek God and follow His guidance in every area of your life, you begin to sparkle and shine and become more and more glorious in all that you are and all that you do.

Right now, set your heart and mind to be willing to change.

You have made great strides in change because you have made it a priority to seek after God. That is one of the most beneficial things you can do to experience a better life.

Are there any other areas coming to mind where you can change for the better? Talk to God about it.

Ready, Set, Seek!

Record your experience with God.

What is your prayer?

What do you believe God is saying to you?

Ready, Set, Seek!

WEEK 2 COMPLETE!

DAY FIFTEEN

ASK GOD FOR HELP

"God is my help in every need. God does my every hunger feed. He walks beside me and guides my way through every moment of the day. I now am humble. I now am true, gentle, kind and loving too...." This is something that my mom would say to herself whenever she felt stressed or was going through a tough time. She meditated all the time, and I heard her muttering and praying and speaking the Word to herself often. It's amazing what kids pick up and how closely they watch their parents. I don't remember being taught this prayer. I just recall her saying it, and I learned it by watching and listening to my mother asking God for help. There was never a time when He failed to come through for her. She always called on Him for help, and He always answered. Whether the prayer was answered through a person, a song, or a tag on someone's car that said, "Jesus loves you," I witnessed Him always coming through for her. He was always rescuing her and making a way out of no way, even in the worst of circumstances. I could feel His presence there in our house or in the car or wherever we were, because she always invited Him in.

Sometimes, we can learn what to do by watching someone else. Sometimes, watching someone else builds faith in us. For many people, seeing is believing. That's what watching my mom's relationship with God did for me. It built my faith in God to know that He always comes through. In my life as an adult, I know this to be true because He does the same for me. One thing I truly believe with everything in me is that God is ready and willing to

help us. I once heard a preacher say that sometimes the simplest prayer is the most effective. This preacher gave an example of one of King David's prayers. David was in such distress that all he could say was "HELP!" God already knew what was going on, and David knew and understood this, so he simply cried "HELP!"
Look at this Psalm of David:

O Lord, you are so good, so ready to forgive,
so full of unfailing love for all who ask for your help.
Listen closely to my prayer, O LORD;
hear my urgent cry.
I will call to you whenever I'm in trouble,
and you will answer me (Psalm 86:5-7, NLT).

God will answer you. It's NOT a question of whether God will answer. It's a question of whether you will ask. His desire to help is a done deal. He is committed to you, and He will respond to your sincere prayer for help. God loves to help. Providing help is a part of His nature. Since the beginning of time, He's been helping mankind: He gave Adam a help meet, He sent the Holy Spirit to be our helper, and so on and so on. He knows we need Him, and He freely gives of Himself to us.

Even through this journey of learning to seek Him, He has promised to help. You can actually pray, "God, help me to seek after you with a pure heart and consistency. Help me to ignore distractions so I can focus on You and really see the benefits of spending time with You." Even if it's something internal that you need help with, such as feelings of depression, loneliness, despair and emptiness. God knows we are flesh (human) and at times we get weak. He wants to help with that, too. God is strong, and He wants you to be strong. All the strength, power, and peace we need are available in His presence. He wants to do amazing things in our lives. Then we can

62

tell others about what He's done so He can get involved in their lives, too.

After David cried out for help, this was his prayer:
You are my strong shield,
and I trust you completely.
You have helped me,
and I will celebrate
and thank you in song (Psalm 28:7, CEV).

Whatever it is you need today, don't be afraid to ask God for it—no matter how big or small. He loves you.

Ready, Set, Seek!

Record your experience with God.

What is your prayer?

What do you believe God is saying to you?

KNOW THAT GOD IS TRUSTWORTHY

Trust God from the bottom of your heart;
don't try to figure out everything on your own.
Listen for God's voice in everything you do, everywhere
you go; he's the one who will keep you on track.
Don't assume that you know it all (Proverbs 3:5-12,
MSG).

I want to start this chapter off with this scripture about trust. Trust is hard, so having some encouragement coupled with a promise from the good book will help. Again, trust is hard. Let's be real. God is invisible, and we have bills and so many other worries, making it difficult to let go and believe that everything will work out fine. But we must do this. When I worry about things and become stressed and anxious about the future, it really doesn't help. Newsflash, right? Worrying does nothing.

Jesus wasn't kidding when He said not to worry about tomorrow. You have enough to deal with today, and you really need to learn to trust God. In my experience, when I let go of the worry and say, "Okay, God. I'm giving this issue over to you, and I'm trusting you to work it out," He always does. I have to talk to myself and tell my emotions to calm down. God works it out when we trust Him. He really is trustworthy, and He always keeps His promises. We don't give Him the credit He deserves. He's never given us a reason to doubt Him. Sure, we have had disappointments, but I'm willing to bet they were self-imposed. Just because we want something a certain way doesn't mean that our way is the best way.

Trusting in God also means trusting Him with the outcome. Like the scripture says, "Trust God from the bottom of your heart; don't try to figure out everything on your own." In this era of advanced technology, with a nation of college graduates and infinite access to DIY YouTube videos, that sounds a bit foreign. Many may say, "What do you mean don't try to figure it out? I'm paid to figure things out. I went to school for years to learn to figure things out." But this relationship is going to require a paradigm shift. We have to learn to walk by faith. We must learn to lean on God and rely on Him for the next step, to depend on Him. Wooooo! That's a stretch, I know. But it's the key to seeing all your dreams come true.

God is adventurous. And having faith in Him is going to require some courage and a sense of adventure. Who wants to live for a boring God who doesn't develop and empower you anyway? God is the ultimate mentor. He's progressive, forward thinking, and a trail blazer. And the awesome thing is He knows how it's all going to turn out, because He knows the ending from the beginning.

This is what God said to a group of His children that were in bondage, far away from home and lost in every conceivable way:

"I know what I'm doing. I have it all planned out—plans to take care of you, not abandon you, plans to give you the future you hope for. When you call on me, when you come and pray to me, I'll listen. When you come looking for me, you'll find me. Yes, when you get serious about finding me and want it more than anything else, I'll make sure you won't be disappointed. God's Decree. I'll turn things around for you" (Jeremiah 29:11-14, MSG).

Once they heard this word, they had to believe it to benefit from it.

Trust is not just a relaxed feeling you have after you gain an understanding that God has your back. It is also obedience or walking in line with the guidance He gives you. If I tell you to meet me at a restaurant so I can buy you lunch, you must show up to receive the free meal. If you show up, God will show up, and He never disappoints. Trust Him with everything.

Ready, Set, Seek!

Record your experience with God.

What is your prayer?

What do you believe God is saying to you?

DAY SEVENTEEN

THE AUTHORITY THAT GOD HAS GIVEN YOU

Being a believer in God does not mean that you become weak. Some people think that, once you become a Christian, you have to settle for a watered-down life and live under everyone's thumb. That is NOT the truth. In reality, being a Christian should be likened to walking around like a spiritual giant. I know that probably sounds weird, because most Christians do not live like that at all. This is unfortunate and disheartening. However, it is probably the case because we have a distorted view of the Person we are following. Jesus was no wimp. When He walked this earth, He was full of power and authority. He knew exactly who He was and what He was on this planet to do. He was not afraid of or intimidated by anyone.

I think when we read the stories about Jesus we sometimes do not comprehend His mission properly. Excuse my choice of words here, but this guy was a beast! He had it together and made it look easy. He was literally walking around healing the sick and raising the dead. Let me repeat; "He raised the DEAD." He calmed storms. He went in a synagogue and saw people using God's house just to make money, and He got so angry that He started turning over tables!

He was not tolerating any foolishness. Jesus walked up to total strangers and said, "Follow me," and they dropped what they were doing and went after him. Jesus was The Man, literally. I believe that God wants us to walk in that same confidence and authority.

Behold, I have given you authority to tread on serpents and scorpions, and over all the power of the enemy, and

69

nothing shall hurt you (Luke 10:19, ESV).

According to the Merriam-Webster Dictionary, the definition of authority is "power to influence or command thought, opinion, or behavior."7 When Jesus said the word "power," He was referring to the Greek word exousía, which means power, authority, dominion, control, sway.8 When I was looking up these words online I saw the image of a tall red man standing in front of a group of blue men. The picture I described represents what you look like in the spirit realm. You are the red man or woman, you stand out and you are full of power. The problem is that you don't know this or maybe don't fully believe it. But if you are a Christian, this is who you are! If you are not a Christian, you can easily change that. It takes ten seconds. All you have to do is say, **"Jesus, come into my heart and forgive my sins. I believe that You died on the cross for me and rose again on the third day. Thank you!"** It's so simple because He did all the hard stuff.

God has given you power. You don't have to put up with anything that is not good and in line with what God's Word says your life should look like. So, when you are seeking God, go boldly, realizing that you have the right to talk to Him, hear His voice, and receive the goodness He has for you. This is your God-given right.
"So whenever we are in need, we should come bravely before the throne of our merciful God. There we will be treated with undeserved kindness, and we will find help" Hebrews 4:16, CEV).

It has nothing to do with where you came from, who your family is, or what you have done or haven't done. This power and authority is God's gift to you. This authority is to be used when bad things are happening. Just like Jesus spoke to the roaring waves of the sea and calmed everything down, you can do that in your life and in the lives of others.

This is the attitude and the posture you should have when you are seeking after God. God honors His Word, and it pleases Him when we honor it by coming to Him like the kings and queens He created us to be.

I'll give you an example. Let's say you are going into your prayer time, and there is a situation at work that's on your mind. You have been mistreated, and you know it isn't right. Here is your chance to use your authority. You can pray and say something like this: "Father, I'm coming boldly to your throne asking for your help and guidance. This situation at work is bothering me, and I want it to stop. Right now, I take authority over whatever negative spirit is influencing Jane to try to make things difficult for me, and I command it to cease in its actions against me. I will have peace at work. I'm gifted to do magnificent work and to do it in joy. I thank You for the authority You have given me to walk all over evil, in Jesus' name."

God already knows what's happening with us. He knows we are human, and we need to talk things out and vocalize our thoughts. He put creative power in words, and just like He used words to create the world and change things, He has given us the ability to do so as well. Use your God-given power.

Ready, Set, Seek!

Record your experience with God.

What is your prayer?

What do you believe God is saying to you?

DAY EIGHTEEN

SAY THANK YOU

Saying "thank you" is a love language to God. Most of us are always asking God for something but are rarely saying thank you. Saying thank you is an art we must get a hold of if we want to see more miraculous things happening in our lives. It's interesting how we thank people for the smallest things—opening a door, serving us food—but we forget to thank God for life, health, strength, etc. He's so sweet to us, even when we don't do the right things, but this is your reminder. Remember to thank Him for all He's done for you.

God is not just a Father. He is also a King, and when you come into the presence of royalty, there are certain customs and practices that must be adhered to. The custom utilized when entering into God's presence is to come with thankfulness and praise. This is what Psalm 100:4 says:

"Enter into his gates with thanksgiving, and into his courts with praise: be thankful unto him and bless his name."

Thankfulness has blessings attached to it. Look at Philippians 4:6-7:

"Don't worry about anything but pray about everything. With thankful hearts offer up your prayers and requests to God. Then, because you belong to Christ Jesus, God will bless you with peace that no one can completely understand. And this peace will control the way you think and feel" (CEV).

I absolutely love this scripture. It pretty much says it all.

1) Don't worry about it.

2) Pray about it.

3) Have a thankful heart as you pray about it. (Find something to be thankful for even though you are feeling some stress and strain.)

4) Know that, because you belong to Christ, God is not going to leave you hanging. He's going to give you the peace you need so you can sleep and work and do what needs to be done while you wait for the solution.

5) People probably won't understand how you are peaceful and still smiling, even under heavy circumstances.

6) Peace will keep your heart, mind, and emotions in the right state.

We need to look at God like He's that super awesome friend that will never let you down. He's like that friend you can tell anything, without judgement, even when you do something stupid. We need to rely on God like that. Have confidence in His love and His loyalty and thank Him for it. He's literally got your front, back, and both sides.

When we are thankful, it increases our ability to receive more because it shows that our hearts are right and humble. There is no pride or entitlement in a thankful heart. For example, when humans feel appreciated, they are motivated to do more. Giving is a byproduct of love, and the appreciation and thankfulness we give inspires more love and more giving. When I give my nieces something and I see their faces light up and express gratitude, it just makes me want to give them everything. Parents experience this often, and God is an awesome Father. Decide to always come to God with thanksgiving and watch the blessings flow.

Ready, Set, Seek!

Record your experience with God.

What is your prayer?

What do you believe God is saying to you?

DAY NINETEEN

ASK GOD FOR WHAT YOU WANT

What do you want? I had to ask myself this question because I got to the place where I was so overworked and so tired that I didn't even know exactly what I wanted. When I had fleeting thoughts about things I thought I wanted, I didn't ask God and use my faith. I was just living day to day. I remember sitting on my couch and hearing God say to me, "What do you want? Ask me." I thought that was so strange. But in hindsight, I realized that He was saying this to me because I was thinking I had to do everything for myself and because that is not how God designed life to work. God wants us to depend on Him and ask for His help and His guidance. Don't get me wrong. He does not want us to be lazy, sitting around waiting for things to magically appear. He wants to be a part of our lives, and He wants to provide for us. He wants to lead and guide us to the best possible way to obtain the best possible life.

I enjoy doing vision boards because it gives a visual of what I am praying for. It gives color to the imagination, and if you can see it and believe it, you can have it. But it begins with God and asking Him for what you want, because He is the source of every good and perfect gift.

Jesus said it best:

"A thief is only there to steal and kill and destroy. I came so they can have real and eternal life, more and better life than they ever dreamed of." (John 10:10, MSG).

Wow, what does that look like to you?

More life, a better life than you ever dreamed of?

Seeking God comes with a promise.
In Psalm 37: 4-5 says:

Delight yourself also in the Lord, and He will give you the desires and secret petitions of your heart.
Commit your way to the Lord [roll and repose each care of your load on Him]; trust (lean on, rely on, and be confident) also in Him and He will bring it to pass (AMPC).

Think about what you truly want, be specific, and ask God for it. As you spend time with Him, He will weave His perfect plan in your heart so that you have the desires that represent God's best for you. He's got you.

Ready, Set, Seek!

Record your experience with God.

What is your prayer?

What do you believe God is saying to you?

DAY TWENTY

REFLECT – HOW HAVE YOU CHANGED?

This chapter is simply about reflecting on the past 19 days and looking at what has happened, what God has done for you, and how you have developed. What have you learned about God? What have you learned about yourself? I know that some amazing things have taken place or are on the horizon. Take a few minutes and write some of these things down and thank God for what He's done and for all the awesome things that are yet to come. Making the decision to be thankful helps you to always be mindful of the gifts and beauty all around you. Thankfulness also opens your capacity to receive more good things.

I also want you to take a moment and pat yourself on the back. Yes! You have been so faithful and consistent. You have taken the steps to live beyond a natural, ordinary, boring life. You have taken a step that has opened the door to your best, most powerful and most beautiful life. I'm so proud of you. This took faith and guts.

Reflect

Take a moment write some notes about your journey:

Ready, Set, Seek!

DAY TWENTY-ONE

FAITHFULNESS – KEEP IT UP

This seek challenge is not meant to end after twenty-one days. It's meant to become your lifestyle. The truth is, we need God every single day of our lives.
The Psalmist wrote:

Your eyes saw my unformed substance, and in Your book all the days [of my life] were written before ever they took shape, when as yet there was none of them (Psalm 139:16, AMPC).

Think of this; God wrote about each day you would live and everything you would do in a book before you were even born. He's already been where you are headed, and you need His guidance to ensure that you are on the right path.
Look at Proverbs 3:5-6 (AMPC):

"Lean on, trust in, and be confident in the Lord with all your heart and mind and do not rely on your own insight or understanding. In all your ways know, recognize, and acknowledge Him, and He will direct and make straight and plain your paths."

I have had so many challenges with being unsure about the right path or the right job to take and the right person or right people to hang around. When I sought God about those things, He made the right decision very plain to see. After all, He knows all things, and He knows exactly what He is doing.

I love Jeremiah 29:11-14, which says:

"'I know what I'm doing. I have it all planned out—plans to take care of you, not abandon you, plans to give you the future you hope for. When you call on me, when you come and pray to me, I'll listen. When you come looking for me, you'll find me. Yes, when you get serious about finding me and want it more than anything else, I'll make sure you won't be disappointed.' God's Decree" (MSG).

Continue seeking the Lord. It's easy to stop after you've gotten what you came for. I encourage you to continue to be faithful, continue being thankful and sharing what has happened to you and how your life has changed. If you haven't seen anything major happen yet, continue and expect to see some awesome things because they are on the way! Share this book. Write me (at the address in the front of this book) and tell me about your experience. Let's spread the word about this amazing God who wants us to have an amazing life. Challenge someone else to seek God today. May God bless you in ways that exceed your greatest expectations as you continue to seek after Him!

Ready, Set, Seek!

Notes

Day 2
1Dictionary.com. www.dictionary.com/browse/seek. Accessed 17 July 2018.
2Bible Hub. www.biblehub.com/greek/2212.htm. Accessed 17 July 2018.

Day 3
3Vocabulary.com. www.vocabulary.com/distraction. Accessed 19 July 2018.
4Vocabulary.com. www.vocabulary.com/preoccupy. Accessed 19 July 2018.
5Vocabulary.com. www.vocabulary.com/focus. Accessed 19 July 2018.

Day 9
6J. Sugarman. "Are There Any Proven Benefits to Fasting?" John Hopkins Heath Review, 3, no.1 (2016): 8-10.

Day 17
7Merriam-Webster Dictionary. www.merriamwebster.com/dictionary/authority. Accessed 25 October 2018.
8 Merriam-Webster Dictionary. www.merriam-webster.com/dictionary/dominion. Accessed 25 October 2018.

God will do exceedingly abundantly more
than you expected.
  2 Chron 7:14
God is calling us to a higher level
with him.
  acquitant   Being more of a light
  supporter
  devoted
Whatever you need - ask Him for it
Don't settle into worrying
Psalm 23: Yahweh is my best friend
and my shepherd - he provides manna
The challenge is to obey God when
you do not know the future -
Follow God's plan. When I try to
figure things out - it does not work out

Matthew 6:33 Seek ye first
21 days - worship & seek me
  20 minutes - worship & prayer

Slow down & focus on what God
  wants to tell me.
Allow Time - Listen - Quiet Yourself
Quiet Place - Bible - Note Pad
Read Scripture